*Dedicated to*
**The Royal Army Chaplains' Department**
*serving the British Army since 1796,*
*who helped me to find the way in war to a Kingdom*
*whose armies cannot be counted*
*and whose sign is the Cross*

Copies of this book obtainable from:

Eastbourne Christian Resource Centre
91-93 Seaside Road
Eastbourne
East Sussex
BN21 3PL

Tel: 01323 732 070

Cover Illustration: *Before I Go* by David Plested, Eastbourne.

# Before I Go

Mark Green

Mark Green asserts the moral right
to be identified as the author of this book

ISBN 1-9-04499-05-8

First published in United Kingdom of Great Britain in 2005 by
Roundtuit Publishing, 32 Cookes Wood, Broompark, Durham DH7 7RL

# CONTENTS

# INTRODUCTION

Originally this publication was to be only the seven papers printed here as part 2, under the title 'Within no walls confined'. They were sparked off by the medical interview recorded at the beginning of that section. I wanted to write down thoughts before my departure about the future of the Church I have served these sixty and more years. Then there came to light the final edition of a diary which had begun in a rough and ready way during the invasion of Normandy in 1944. Later I tidied it up for publication in *None had Lances*, the regimental history of the 24th Lancers, whose chaplain I was throughout the Normandy campaign. Some fifteen years ago I rewrote it in the form in which it is printed here, adding some reflections on the moral and pastoral questions thrown up by serving as a chaplain to armed forces.

I have called this part **Finding the Way** because I went into the army and to Normandy as a young priest ordained for only three years, after training that was minimal. I scraped through Oxford's Honours Theology degree with a 'third', after being away for much of my last year as a cadet at Sandhurst. I should have been at Cuddesdon for two years, but my bishop (who hated theological colleges) ordained me after two months. I can't say I was heartbroken at not being able to take any more exams, with war raging and (in 1940) an invasion of this country a real possibility. Nevertheless I had a lot of learning to do, and I was hugely fortunate in the people who supplied some of it, mainly the senior chaplains and commanding officers under whom I served.

The Royal Army Chaplains' Department is one of the oldest corps in the British Army. In a sense I was born into it, because in 1917 my father was a serving chaplain, and for the first thirteen years of my life I grew up in army environments like Aldershot and Tidworth -even for two years in the Tower of London. During my own war service I was fortunate in having senior chaplains who were both strongly demanding and pastorally sensitive. I had not reckoned with having commanding officers who exercised more power over their chaplains than any bishop would dare to exercise today over priests in his diocese. But this came across as a terrific stimulant, not as a threat. Colonel Mike Aird (9th Lancers) and then Colonel WAC Anderson (17/21st Lancers) commanded the 24th Lancers in my time with them. Both expected the highest standards of ministry from their chaplain, just as they expected total dedication from their subordinate officers. The young officers, especially, quite near my own age, taught me a lot without trying to do so. They themselves were taught that the unforgivable sin was to put their own comfort, convenience or safety before that of their men. I came to love and respect them and to see in them a model for all Christian ministry, ordained or lay. (Perhaps they would have been rather surprised by this, not least after the occasional letting -down-of the hair). In general, from the commanding officer downwards, and including not only the officers but the tank crews they commanded, I was given a lot to live up to, and I have been grateful to them all my life, even if I have fallen below their standards of duty. Maybe that old fashioned word needs reviving in our time.

The seven papers entitled **Within No Walls Confined** were written years later than the Normandy Diary; but form a natural sequel because, for me, finding the way turned out to be outside the walls of gathered Christian communities. That does not alter the fact that my own faith has been ceaselessly nourished within various walls. It isn't a question of either/or. It's worth quoting the whole of William Cowper's verse (from the hymn 'Jesus where'er they people meet')

For thou, within no walls confined,
Inhabitest the humble mind;
Such ever bring thee where they come,
And going, take thee to their home.

All these seven papers say that there is no future in retreating behind the walls of the parish church, no security in 'establishment', or ecclesiastical structures. Everything that I most dearly believe is summed up in the last paper, no 6, 'From the House of Kings to the Courts of Heaven'. It is significant that that Christmas letter received a warm response from a mixed bunch of people, including those who do not share my stance over homosexuality or women priests. I found this profoundly encouraging. There is a way forward. On the Christian Way there always is!

I have already made it clear that these writings spread over a period of some sixty years owe much to other people. I could not have put them together without the advice of Dr Richard Ralph, my trustee and literary executor, and I could not have coped with the technology required without the help of Mary Peck of Eastbourne Parish Church, who has typed and retyped numerous pages. David Plested took great trouble to design a cover that fitted in with the theme of the book, looking beyond what is seen. I would also add Nicholas Reade, now Bishop of Blackburn, who as Vicar and Rural Dean of Eastbourne, 1988 to 1997, gave me great encouragement as a retired priest on his staff, and his successor Canon Charles Lansdale, who has generously saved me (so far) from mental decline by encouraging regular preaching to an intelligent, demanding congregation. To all of them my heartfelt thanks

MARK GREEN

9th April 2005

# FINDING THE WAY
## A WAR DIARY

# Monday, 5th June, 1944

We embarked for the invasion of Normandy at Southampton on Thursday, 1st June, in many ways like Abraham, who "went out not knowing whither he went". We could have added to "whither" the words "whether" and "when", but we hoped somebody knew.   In fact, we pushed out into Southampton Water, and lay at anchor over what seemed a very long weekend, part of an enormous gathering of ships of all sizes.   All the time there were rumours as to when we might go.

On Sunday, 3rd June, (Trinity Sunday) I went round various ships in a motor boat to take impromptu communion services.   Back on board my own ship, an American tank landing ship, the Captain and the O.C. Troops gathered everybody to hear various messages. There was one from the King, others from Generals Eisenhower and Montgomery.   The Captain asked me if there was anything from the Church.   I pulled out of my pocket a letter which the Archbishop of Canterbury (William Temple) had sent to all the invasion chaplains. This was not exactly a "Cry-God-for-Harry-England-and-St-George" sort of letter but I read it out, suppressing references to chaplains, which had the effect of making the hearers (ordinary soldiers) seem much holier than they really were.   However, it went down well, especially the bit about helping to restrain the men's passions and lusts in the hour of victory.   The thought of victory, not to mention the passions and lusts which were evidently to come in its train, was quite encouraging to them.

The mood generally during these days is a mixture of excitement, uncertainty and relief:   excitement, because most of us are young enough to be excited by adventure;   uncertainty, because from the

1

time we embarked until today there have only been rumours about the date of D-Day;   and relief, because at last something must be about to happen.   The 24th Lancers, to whom I am attached (in more senses than one) have been training for this invasion for a long time, and however much of an ordeal it may be, there is a desire to get on with it.   But I find no bloodthirsty "up-and-at-'em" attitude.   Now at last there is some definite news.   The sea has calmed down this afternoon, and we are to sail for Normandy this evening.

### Tuesday, 6th June : D-Day

We left Southampton Water about 6.30 last night.   All night the LST (Tank Landing Ship) moved slowly, but rolled uneasily, the sea not so calm after all.   I shared a cabin with a young American naval officer and somebody called Bill Downes, of the Columbia Broadcasting System, and slept fitfully for a few hours.   In the early morning there was no sight of land.

As far as the eye could see there were ships of all shapes and sizes, ploughing along very slowly.   This extraordinary armada might have been preparing for an old-fashioned review by the King, or taking part in some bizarre kind of cross-channel race to see who could go slowest.   Not until midday did we see the coast of Normandy, though we were meant to have landed long before this.   About three miles offshore we anchored.   Nobody knew what was happening, least of all the American captain of our ship.   It seemed incongruous to be having a rather good lunch;   in fact there was nothing else to do.

During the afternoon the regiment tried to land its tanks from some of the LSTs.   This involved opening huge doors in the bows of the ships a mile or two offshore, and the tanks then driving on to a contraption known as a "Rhino Ferry". This appeared to be a series of barrels lashed together, the whole propelled by an outboard motor. It all looked – indeed was – highly risky. The trouble began when the Rhino started to move, because the steering arrangements seem non-existent, resulting in aimless and dangerous drifting. One of these Rhinos, with 24th Lancer tanks and crews aboard, drifted in to shore just in time for a German plane to drop a bomb beside them, whereupon, to their relief, they drifted out to sea again.

As the evening wore on, I realised that we were not going to land that night. For hours we had strained our eyes to see what we could on shore; through binoculars we had seen men and vehicles landing and the beaches full of activity. Inland there were numerous clouds of smoke and the noise of explosions. Near our ship *Warspite* and other battleships were firing their guns constantly at targets on land. German planes started bombing us without doing much damage, though one of the men on our ship was wounded. The Captain gave orders to the ship to "make smoke" as a protection against aircraft. It made smoke all right, but most of it seemed to be inside rather than outside the ship. Uneasily, we prepared to spend another night with our friendly American hosts.

### Wednesday, 7th June: D + 1

At least the long delay (nearly a week since we embarked) gave me time to think; time also to pray – though, as so often happens, when there is the time there is not the capacity. Perhaps all I mean is that there is not the opportunity to do it in the conventional way taught at theological colleges, but there is certainly desire to pray, and that is in the end the vital thing.

The time of waiting before battle is a time to face fear. For me this was a very real thing. Blessed (or cursed?) with a vivid imagination, I could all too easily see myself being torn apart by some bomb or mine, and feel the pain and horror of it. The answer, I told myself, was to divert the mind to something more hopeful and constructive; easier said than done, but on the other hand it is good that one should face death calmly and hopefully. As for so many people, it is not the fact of death that horrifies me, but the possible manner of one's dying.

I was aware during those days of another consideration. It was not much more than four years previously, in the early months of the war, that I had left Sandhurst, to which I had been drafted as an officer cadet on the outbreak of war. After I had been there for two months, preparing to be commissioned into the Oxford and Buckinghamshire Light Infantry, the Government added theological students to the list of reserved occupations – i.e., those exempted from conscription. I need not have taken this up, but I did, and went back to Oxford to complete my degree, and then on to ordination via a very short spell at Cuddesdon Theological College. I told myself at the time that I would do more good as a priest than as a combatant officer. This might, or might not, have been true. In any case, it was not really "either – or", but could have been first one and then, if I survived, the other. But, looking back, I have to admit that there was an element of cowardice in the decision. Later, when I saw the Dunkirk casualty lists, and the names of some of my fellow cadets who had been killed in action, there was a feeling of self-loathing. By what right had I taken this shortcut to fulfilling my "career", when they had unquestioningly given up theirs?

Now, having got back into the army by a different route and in a different role, there was the chance of expiation. Or was there? The past can be forgiven, but can never be undone. Yet was I not right to think that that tremendous assault on Hitler's Europe gave me the chance to say to God, "I'm sorry for that failure, that betrayal. Thank you for this chance as a priest to minister to people in extreme need and danger, and please help me not to fail this time"? Well, it sounds horribly priggish, but it does represent the better side of me which, thank God, is what He sees in all of us.

*****

These ruminations were terminated by our LST actually moving in towards the shore – albeit slowly and with frequent stops. But at last we got to within a few hundred yards of the beaches. The big moment had come. The ship opened its doors, the tanks drove out into the water, and on to the beach. I was with Douglas Aitken, the 24th Lancers medical officer, in his armoured half-tracked vehicle. As we moved out into the water in our turn, the engine spluttered and failed. Anti-climax! Something wrong with the valve-spring, so the driver said. Nothing could be done about it, and on we plunged into the water, the engine making horrible noises. All around us, vehicles were struggling ashore, tanks, lorries, jeeps, scout cars, motorcycles – and masses of men. Some vehicles had come to grief in the water, some on shore. Ours managed to stagger on. We went in the direction of the rendezvous, about a mile beyond the village of Le Hamel. Here vehicles came to be sorted into regimental groups. Each unit landed from a large number of ships, and in a number of places, frequently not the ones planned.

All the invasion chaplains had been issued with a two-stroke motorcycle. I got mine off the half-track and pop-pop-popped off to try to get news of where the rest of the regiment was, for 'B' Squadron had landed the night before (on D-Day) and was said to be in action. Eventually I found them, and very pleased with themselves they were for having outstripped the rest of us; Bunny Leather, one of the young troop leaders, had actually shot up some German tanks.

It was not till 11 pm on the day after D-Day that the whole of the regimental assault party was ashore, with its vehicles assembled and de-waterproofed. Even the doctor's crippled half-track had arrived, ignominiously towed and quite useless, except that it provided me and others with somewhere to sleep.

Our harbouring place for the night was on some high ground looking down over the invasion beaches. Far out to sea were ships of all sizes, with more always coming over the horizon. The Luftwaffe was still busy, and the air full of red tracer bullets and coloured Verey lights. We spent an uneasy night because of the noise of the air-raids and the frequent 'crump' of bombs; and because our foothold was still far from secure. When you know that the German army, a few miles away, would like to push you into the sea and drown you, and is in fact trying to do so, your sleep is not easy.

# Thursday, 8th June:  D + 2

The plan for our Brigade (8th Independent Armoured) was to form a mobile column, led by the 24th Lancers, to penetrate seventeen miles inland to a place called Villers Bocage.   This morning the column set off, but we never got anywhere near Villers Bocage.   (It did not in fact fall for another week or two.)

Because of the trouble with the doctor's half-track I was left behind to get it mended, while he went on in the column in his proper place with Regimental Headquarters.   I did not however get left behind as much as I feared, because there wasn't much behind to get left in, as our progress was so painfully slow.   I spent the morning dealing with the LAD (REME Light Aid Detachment) and called at Brigade HQ.   Periodically we made cups of tea or had other nourishment from the 24-hour packs with which we were supplied.   Most of this seemed to be on the meat lozenge system, or things that you squeezed out of tubes;   and (best of all) small tins of self-heating soup – a minor miracle.

During the afternoon the Regiment began to have its first casualties. Alick Poole, our first officer casualty, was killed by an explosive bullet which struck his steel helmet while he was standing in the turret of his tank.   Stray snipers, perched in trees, were a real menace in these early days.   We had quite a number of other casualties, and I found it worrying not to be able to be in all the places where one should have been.   I was beginning to learn the difficulties of being padre to armoured units in battle.   One of the difficulties centred around transport. My flock were widely scattered.   The two-stroke motorcycle was quite useless in battle;   my official vehicle was an Austin utility van (still somewhere out at sea) and I tended to hop along in other people's vehicles, or "borrow" them awhile, as an alternative to wandering around on foot. As no-one seemed to know which was the "front" or "back" of this battle, you were liable to get blown to pieces by tank guns firing from all directions, and as likely to be despatched by your own side as by the Nazis.

I was in no doubt that I should find a way of solving this one, and already had my eye on a rather neat-looking armoured scout car. It was just the job for me, except for a gun mounted on top, which I soon disposed of. The duty of the padre was to be where the action was, one way or another. For my part, I found it slightly surprising that I had this great anxiety to be there.

### Friday, 9<sup>th</sup> – Sunday, 11<sup>th</sup> June

A hellish few days. I knew little about the big picture, but guessed it was the same on other parts of the invasion front. It was really a miracle that we were still in Normandy, and not smashed to bits and driven into the sea.

We (8<sup>th</sup> Armoured Brigade, including 24<sup>th</sup> Lancers, in support of 50<sup>th</sup> Northumbrian division) had been holding a high position identified on the map only as "Pt 103". But Point 103 became a poignant symbol for all of us; really it was just a bit of rising ground a few miles from the beaches. The more wooded part was about half a mile square, and it was here that we beat off attacks from the Panzer Lehr, a crack German tank division which had driven 90 miles from Chartres to get at us; also from the famous 12<sup>th</sup> SS Panzer (Hitler Jugend) Division, with their fanatically brave boys who counted it an honour to die for their Führer.

All through those days I based myself at the 24L Regimental Aid Post with our medical officer, Douglas Aitken. The Regimental Aid Post was nothing more than a bit of space in an orchard on the top of this literally blasted hill. Douglas had been working night and day on streams of casualties, far too many to deal with. So it was a case of doing what he could for the most badly wounded, and trying to get them and the others away to the Advanced Dressing Station a few miles back, as soon as possible. But we were desperately short of ambulances and stretcher-carrying jeeps, and the wounded piled up. Douglas was operating in appallingly difficult conditions; e.g., doing what he could for a man who had lost both legs, working in the dark by the dimmed light of a torch, with a gas-cape rigged up between the branches as shelter from the rain – not much like the Edinburgh hospital where he had trained only a few years before. Yet somehow he has triumphed over this fearful test of his stamina and skill, in spite of no sleep, hardly any food, constant terror, and the agony of those lying mutilated around us. Over and over again came the whine of mortar bombs, mounting to a crescendo, and then the "crump" of explosion. Bits of jagged metal did their horrible work on bodies until then strong and fit, and more people were carried into our RAP.

I soon saw that my most useful role would be to do what I could to speed up the evacuation of our casualties, for in many cases their hope of survival depended on surgery that could not possibly be done in the middle of an orchard, in the dark and the rain. I therefore took a jeep – nobody seemed to be in the mood to say "Hi, what are you doing? That's mine" – and drove across fields and farm tracks to find the Advanced Dressing Station between us and the beaches. God knows how I found it, because normally my sense of direction is so bad that I would get lost trying to find Trafalgar Square at the end of Whitehall – I would get to the wrong end. Anyway, I found this medical haven and poured out my soul to the Commanding Officer of the ADS, Colonel Arnold of the Royal Army Medical Corps.

I must have seemed both desperate and genuine because he gave orders that every available vehicle was to be rounded up. He told me to lead this convoy of ambulances and stretcher-bearing jeeps back to Point 103, where I could imagine it bringing tears of delight mixed with exhaustion to Douglas Aitken's eyes. Colonel Arnold said he would come with me in the leading jeep. In fact, he did a lot more than that: he went on from Point 103 into St Pierre, a village in front of our position, and personally evacuated 37 wounded while a battle was raging in the village the whole time.

*****

Mention of St Pierre reminds me of an escapade late one Friday night. Shortly before midnight I gathered from our Commanding Officer (Colonel 'Wac' Anderson – more about him later) that he was sending six lorries down into St Pierre. 'C' Squadron was installed in one end of the village, having put in an attack with the 8th Durham Light Infantry at 5.30 that evening. Now the tanks needed refuelling and the men needed rations. Colonel Wac agreed to my going with them, because I hadn't seen 'C' Squadron for some time. So off I went in the leading 3-tonner with Squadron Sergeant-Major Clayton. What endless sessions he and I had had in England about his domestic problems, but no time for them now. We drove through cornfields and on rough tracks (and once down a perilous bank by mistake), gradually losing our sense of direction – not that I ever really knew where we were going. Finally we hit a narrow road and went along it until we came to a road block at the entrance to a village.

The night was now still, firing had stopped, the moon was up, and it felt rather ghostly. We got out and surveyed the road block. SSM Clayton said, "OK, I'll have a go", and drove the lorry full tilt at it. There was a blinding flash, a loud explosion, and the back wheels of the lorry were blown off. Clayton was all right, but I thought, "O God, in a moment we're going to be prisoners", and I got the other five lorries moving backwards up the narrow lane, fearing we had got to the wrong village, occupied by the enemy and not by our people. In preparation for going "into the bag" I tore up all the maps and papers I could lay hands on (later much regretted).

While this was going on, and our lorries were milling about like performing elephants, a jeep suddenly appeared from the rear, with an angry English officer. "What the hell do you think you're doing?", he called. I said, truthfully, that I had no idea. Seeing my clerical collar through the darkness he cooled down slightly. "Padre", he said, "this is an invasion, not a Sunday School picnic, and anyway why are you tearing up those maps?" Like a politician dodging awkward questions, I asked him which village this was, and learnt that it was indeed St Pierre, and that we had just gone over a mine. Calm being restored, we went on into the village, and found 'C' Squadron tanks. Their crews were very surprised to see us, and, having heard the commotion at the entrance to the village, were relieved that it was us and not the Germans; very pleased also to see that we had brought them food and fuel, though I could feel them thinking that if it had needed the regimental chaplain to bring these things, the situation must be even more desperate than they feared. Clearly, they didn't believe that I had come just to see them. I found it a bit hard to believe myself, in view of the bother we had had in finding them.

Having had a word with those who were not trying to sleep, I went off to the RAP of the 8th Durham Light Infantry to see if any of our casualties were there. In fact, the damaged farmhouse serving as their RAP was crammed with DLI casualties. By the light of a lantern their doctor was working on his knees, with the wounded groaning all round him, some unconscious, some sleeping fitfully, some dying and a few dead. It seemed impossible to evacuate them, but when dawn broke I acquired a 3-ton lorry into which we loaded as many as we could of those who looked as though they might survive the journey. So back we went toward the Advanced Dressing Station, via Point 103, where the battle was still going on.

The path back to the Bayeux main road had tracer bullets whizzing across it from each side, and as I was surveying the scene doubtfully the Brigadier (Cracroft) suddenly appeared. He chided us for stopping and told us to crack on. "You'll be all right", he said, "Just push on". At this moment the young medical lance-corporal I had brought with me said, "Padre, I think we ought to push on. Some of the chaps in the lorry aren't too good; if we don't get them treated soon they'll be dead". Feeling much ashamed, I told the driver to go on as fast as he could without jolting the 3-tonner too much, and, just as the Brigadier had predicted, we got through safely and unshipped our pathetic human cargo at the Advanced Dressing Station. One had died on the way. Quite an eventful night.

\*\*\*\*\*

After breakfast and a wash at the ADS I made my way back to Point 103 and our own Regimental Aid Post.

Friday had merged into Saturday – and Saturday merged into Sunday – so that it became impossible to remember exactly what had happened and when. But on that Saturday I was shaken by one experience. Late that morning I was at the 4th/7th Royal Dragoon Guards Regimental Aid Post on the other side of the hill from ours, talking to Hedleigh Davies, their chaplain, when one of their tanks drove up and stopped. The crew tumbled out looking completely shattered. They explained that they had been shot up, and their tank commander, a young subaltern named Geoffrey Mitchell, was dead inside the turret; would we please get him out. (I had known Geoffrey during our training in England, and in fact I had had a hand in preparing him for Confirmation.)

Hedleigh and I asked the crew to drive the tank to some more secluded spot, and then he and I got down to our gruesome task. Somehow we got him out, though never before had we seen such a ghastly sight, and several times we nearly gave up. Later in the day, Hedleigh having been called away, I buried Geoffrey. As I said the words of the Burial Service I was in tears, feeling physically and emotionally at breaking point.

I found these burials among the most difficult things I had to do. For a variety of reasons it was essential that they be done with as much reverence, dignity and efficiency as possible, but the physical part of it was necessarily crude and makeshift. All we could do was bury the body in a shallow grave, mark it with a wooden cross, with the name and unit written on, and try to record a map reference for those who had to do the tidying up later. We did all this as well as we could, but it was impossible not to reflect sometimes that this was not really the task for which the bishop thought he was ordaining us, or which we thought we were accepting. Over and over again during those extraordinary days, I was having to revise my ideas about priesthood.

*****

After nearly a week in action I was reflecting on the tremendous battering we were all taking, not only physically but emotionally. If it had been only lack of sleep, lack of proper food, constant physical effort, it would have been bad enough. But the shock of seeing friends killed or terribly injured, and the inevitable fear that this would soon be one's own fate, put a strain on the resources of the mind and spirit that soon became overwhelming. Perhaps it was natural and even right that the chaplain in battle should have been subjected to this as much as, or even more than, his combatant friends, but for them, especially the youngest ones, the strain could reach terrible proportions. I had a glimpse of this one Sunday evening. Donald Drake, one of our young subalterns, had been in action all day during our counter-attack on St Pierre. He was hit on the forehead by a rifle bullet, and his tank disabled, but he continued to fight the tank until his ammunition ran out. He brought his crew back unhurt, despite enemy machine-gun fire, then took over another tank and returned to his old position, fighting till darkness, when he successfully recovered his first, disabled, tank. For quite a lot of the day, with his wireless aerial out of action, he had been stuck out in front of our position without means of communication or knowledge of what was going on.

I was wandering about on foot later that evening when I met Donald, and on greeting him he burst into tears, and sobbed.   I didn't at that time know what I have recorded above, but it didn't need great sensitivity to know that he was going through hell.

Fortunately, I had by now "acquired" the armoured scout car mentioned earlier.  Fortunately also, I saw the commanding officer, Colonel 'Wac' Anderson, at this moment and told him about Donald.   He agreed to let me deal with him, so I got him into the scout car, pulled the hatch over our heads, and told the driver to make for the Advanced Dressing Station at Martragny.   Here I sought out the blessed Colonel Arnold (by this time in my mind a sort of fairy-godmother-cum-patron-saint) and asked him to look after Donald for 48 hours, give him food and the chance to sleep. Two days later he re-appeared as a new man, and a week or two later it was announced that he had been given an "immediate" award of the Military Cross.   Donald was, and is, an example of true courage. Weak people are defeated and broken and give up.  The brave also are defeated and broken and give up – and then go on.

### Sunday night, 11<sup>th</sup> June

Some time in the evening Ted Webb's tank was hit and burst into flames.  "Brewed up" is the current expression for this horrible and frequent happening.   I buried his charred remains next day – everyone very subdued as we thought of poor Winifred, his wife. But I spent a lot of this Sunday night driving an ambulance between our own Aid Post and a Casualty Collecting Post between us and the Advanced Dressing Station.   On one trip, returning from the Casualty Collecting Post to Point 103, at about 11 pm, driving past a vehicle which had been hit and was blazing furiously, my ambulance suddenly also burst into flames as if in sympathy.   I thought we must have been hit, though I had heard nothing.   Where was the fire extinguisher?   Frenzied search yielding nothing, I was about to leave the (empty) ambulance to its fate when a real ambulance driver in the vehicle ahead of me saw what was happening, ran back, and put the flames out with his own extinguisher.   It had caught fire apparently through some mechanical defect.   Anyway, with things bursting into flames all around, one more little flare-up didn't seem to matter.

All through this night Dr Douglas Aitken was treating casualties in the worst possible conditions, and I was still doing my ferrying job. Odd how in all the talks we were given back in England about "the chaplain's role in battle", nobody seemed to foresee this crying need to get casualties away immediately and the difficulties of doing it; and even if they had, the padre was hardly the most obvious person to do it.   After landing on D+1, I lost count of the different types of vehicle I had to drive.   I think it must have been the grace of Holy Orders which enabled me, a complete idiot with things mechanical, to coax most of them into motion.

### Monday, 12<sup>th</sup> June:  D + 6

Difficult to realise it was only a week today that we sailed from Southampton; it seems like a lifetime.  This was another day of great activity, with the Regiment (24L) deployed in positions forward of Point 103, observing eastwards.

It was on this day that Lieut. Kenneth Wareham finished his war for the time being.   Kenneth – a Woodard School (Denstone) product, aged 21 – was a great help to me in my work with the 24th Lancers in Bridlington last year, and since then in other places.   He is a strongly believing but unassuming Christian, the kind of person who makes our faith authentic and attractive.   The general run of officers is sympathetic, and many of them have gone out of their way to help me.   Many would say, if pushed, that they believe in God, but somewhere, and God alone knows exactly where it is, there is a line which separates the sympathetic believer from the committed Christian disciple.  Kenneth has certainly crossed that line.

Now he was in trouble.   On this day, when the Regiment was engaging German anti-tank guns and tank gunfire from Fontenoy, forward of our position, some German helmets were seen in one of the trenches.   Kenneth Wareham went forward with others to investigate, and while the others mounted guard along the top of the trench, Kenneth with considerable courage leapt in, waving his revolver and shouting, "Surrender, you bastards".   (If this language sounds incompatible with his Christian beliefs, it was in fact as meaningless as the way some people, at the other end of the emotional scale, call you "Darling".)   Anyway, about a dozen German soldiers emerged with their hands up, a tough lot from Panzer Lehr Division.   So far he had been lucky, but later Kenneth went forward to investigate a German armoured car which appeared to have been knocked out.   As he and his wireless officer made their way along a hedge there was suddenly a terrific burst of automatic fire just behind him, and he felt as though he had been hit by a sledgehammer.   In fact his left arm was shattered above and below the elbow.   I saw him when he was brought into our RAP, whence he was speedily evacuated.   Later it was touch and go as to whether they amputated the arm.  Miraculously, it was saved – and, even better, he married the charming nurse who looked after him in hospital back in England.

## Wednesday, 14th June:  D + 8

A respite today, as we were pulled back a few miles, the first break after seven days of continuous fighting and very little sleep.  It was also the first chance I had since landing of holding any kind of service.  I organised an impromptu memorial service for our friends who had been killed in these last few days, and followed it with a celebration of holy communion.  One of the difficulties which I hadn't thought of before was the need to keep the number attending such services down to a reasonable limit – not a problem that church life in England had prepared me for.  Of course, these services had to be in the open air – where else was there? – and the Colonel, though extremely sympathetic and helpful to me in every possible way, was not too keen on having a sizable chunk of his regiment wiped out by aircraft attack while worshipping God, so somehow I had to prevent congregations from being a visible target for enemy planes.

## Saturday, 24th June

The answer is, of course, a lot of services for small groups of people, and since last Sunday I have taken about ten services wherever and whenever things were sufficiently calm.

Everything had to be a bit ad hoc:  using for an altar an ammunition box, a packing case, the tailboard of a lorry, or the bonnet of a jeep. Communion services had to be shortened, and prayers often extemporised. Hymn-singing can be a painful pitfall, especially for a small group. I usually pitch the tune too high or too low, resulting in a musical shambles; so normally no hymns now, until bigger services are possible.

What a stern test it is to lead worship without all the 'props' that can in fact cushion one against reality. As for sermons, using a carefully constructed manuscript is impossible and pointless, even if there was a chance of preparing one. You just have to say something briefly to try to light up a word or verse or theme from the Bible with meaning for the extraordinary life-and-death kind of existence we are all leading so precariously. (But in the long run is it all that different back at home in a supposedly peacetime existence?) At least this approach seems to work, in the sense that people listen as though they are hearing it for the first time – as indeed many are.

The barriers are down. There is no hiding behind formality, robes, beautiful music and buildings, elaborate liturgies, even though I would seek to justify these things when they are used well. And when friends are being killed and injured around you, the Eucharist springs to life as never before, because at the heart of it is sacrifice. Theologically I expect I am way off course in thinking that our offering of our bodies and blood is akin to Jesus' sacrifice of His Body and Blood. Of course, His sacrifice is unique. But here the connexion jumps out and hits you. Perhaps theology has to be written not only in ink in lecture rooms, but in blood on battlefields.

## Tuesday, 27th June:  D + 21

Doug Aitken (M.O.) was called over to one of our tanks this evening after a message "I think Corporal ---------- is dead" had been received. He found the crew standing at the front looking sheepish;  down the side of the tank, near the back, this wretched fellow was squatting, and next to him was the cooker, still burning.  His hands were in his pockets, and he was very dead.  On examination the doctor decided that the accidental discharge of one round of machine gun from the neighbouring tank (one of ours) killed him straight out.  The doc tells Pip, acting Squadron Leader, and he flares up: "He's dead, and all bloody day from bloody dawn he sits up there and fights against the Boche, all bloody day;  and the poor bugger comes in and gets shot while brewing up his first cup of tea of the day.  OK, sorry, Doc".

This describes perfectly how many of us feel in these moments of horror, mental pain, and fierce anger.  There is so much that is totally inexplicable, like this event, which makes any sermon about a loving God seem like a sick joke.  Really, of course, Pip's outburst is not a sign of atheism, coarseness, foul temper, hatred, or anything like that.  It is much more a sign of goodness, of loyalty to and love of friends.  "This", he was saying, "is how our world is at present, a bloody awful mess;  but we long for something better, more beautiful, loving and rational."  This is surely a sign of hope, which would be totally contradicted if army chaplains went around blessing guns, and exhorting soldiers to ever greater deeds of blood-lust.  Nothing would discredit us more quickly, and most of all in the eyes of people like Pip.

## Wednesday, 28th June

Fortunately there are lighter moments. I heard today that during one of the short respites since D-Day 'Ginger' Smith, co-driver of one of our tanks, started the stove and put the dixie on for tea. Ginger, who was always preaching hygiene, went off to relieve himself, came back and tested the temperature of the water with his finger. The others all yelled at him, but it still made a lovely mug of tea. The next morning the crew got all the hammers from the tool kit and the large supply of biscuits they hadn't eaten, and hammered them to powder on the top of the tank tracks, which were clean and shiny after running on wet grass. Ginger got his vest – he swore it was clean – and mixed the powdered biscuit with water to make it a soggy mass, spread it out on his vest, and topped it with jam. He then rolled it up and boiled it in a dixie. Apparently it made an excellent roly-poly and tasted as good as a Christmas pudding. The British soldier always was, and still is, wonderfully adaptable.

## 4th July

During one of the lulls which, thank God, occur from time to time, I was chatting to the crew of one of the 'A' Squadron's tanks. Pastoral visitation – to use theological college jargon – is easy under these conditions: no knocking on the door, no awkward explaining why you've come, no defensiveness from those visited (What have we done wrong? Why has the vicar come to see us?). This lot waded straight in with a big theological question: "Padre, do you believe the saying that if the bullet has your number on it, you've had it?"

"No, I think it's a load of rubbish."

"Why?"

"Because I can't believe God spends his time deciding that one of us shall be killed, somebody else wounded, and another one come through without a scratch. If you happen to be in the path of a bomb or a bullet, well, that's it. But that is not the same as saying God put you there." I could see this disconcerted them a bit. There is, after all, a sort of cosy security in the fatalist's creed. Perhaps I seemed to them to be opening up a freer but even more dangerous universe than the one where you can only wait with bowed head for the worst to happen.

But they persevered bravely. Tom, who had always been to the fore in discussions in England, said, "Then you don't believe that God answers prayer?" He explained that people back home were praying for him in church. "So far," he said, with a smile as though he only half believed it, "it seems to have worked."

O God, please let me not destroy whatever faith these boys have. Please let me not turn them away with theological riddles. "Yes", I said, "it has worked, true prayer always will work, and whether you live or die it will make a difference to you, a big difference, so tell them to keep on praying."

At this moment a call came for the crew to attend a briefing by the Squadron Leader. "See you again", they said as they went. I certainly hope I do.

# 7th July

I am spending a day or two at the newly-opened XXX Corps rest camp, a really imaginative – and compassionate – effort on somebody's part, which Lancers are greatly appreciating as and when they can get to it.

It gives me a chance to reflect on the priest's role, in the light of the four weeks and a bit since we landed in Normandy.  My preparation for ordination in 1940 – to call it 'training' would be stretching words too far – was a couple of short terms at Cuddesdon.  I suspect that in the thirty-one days since D-Day there is the equivalent of about a year at a theological college, if I could but distil these overwhelming experiences of ministry into clear lessons.  I will set them down under several headings in the order in which they occur to me.

## (1)  A HUMAN BEING

In battle the barriers are down.  For the priest, like everybody else here, there are no pretences that can't easily be seen through.  You are exposed for what you are.  For example, you may try to hide fear.  But as everyone else is doing the same, we can see through each other, and realise that being afraid doesn't matter;  it is what you do in spite of being afraid.

In the Royal Army Chaplains' Department no-one can sink lower in rank than Captain.  Few rise any higher;  but I read somewhere that the chaplain's three 'pips' are as much of a barrier as a rectory with a long drive and a lodge at the gate.  This is rubbish – in battle anyway.  There is no built-in deference to the chaplain because of rank, and it is doubtful even if there is much deference to his calling and authority as a priest.  It depends who you are and what you are.  In the stress we are undergoing, people see you as you are – a human being – for better or worse, for better _and_ worse.  We are really stripped naked, sometimes literally so, but it is no use worrying, or feeling ashamed or guilty because one is seen to be much less than perfect. God, after all, sees us that way, and out here I think people prefer to do so;   not because they are unkind, but because a real human being speaks more convincingly about God than some sort of ecclesiastical stereotype.

## (2)   SERVANT

It is clear in these Normandy battles that if the chaplain is not prepared to do the most menial tasks he had better go home to a more structured (but less real) existence where a priest is a priest is a priest. Very few of the things I have found myself doing in the past month come into any recognisable category of priestly tasks. Scraping bodies out of tanks, driving ambulances, making tea for the wounded or the exhausted, getting hold of things like soap, toothpaste, writing paper for soldiers short of these things, helping to dig graves, acting as a messenger-boy – for none of these tasks did the Bishop of Gloucester think he was ordaining me as a priest those three years ago.

It is no use saying, "I wasn't ordained for this". Faced with the realities of life and death, there are no neat demarcation lines separating the spiritual from the material. The most famous chaplain of the 1914-1918 War, Geoffrey Studdart-Kennedy, said, "About purely spiritual work – it is all muddled and mixed". How right he was.

One thing worries me about this:   I find myself putting a sort of wartime gloss on this situation, as if saying, "Well, I have to do these things even if I wasn't ordained to do them, because of the extraordinary conditions under which we are living". The disconcerting thing is that God may be saying that in these extraordinary conditions there is the possibility of finding an aspect of ordained ministry which is just as valid in what we are pleased to call "ordinary" times.  Washing smelly feet (John 13) wasn't very obviously a priestly function, any more than getting dead bodies out of tanks is.  Yet that was the opening scene in the final act revealing the true nature of divine glory.  I can't probe deeper into this at the moment, but I know I am on to something very important for the true understanding of the priest's role, whether in war or peace. And I make a mental note to look up the Greek word *diakonia* in a lexicon (if I ever see one again!) because I remember hearing a sermon as an undergraduate on the theme that this word, to do with service, and from which we get our title of deacon, literally means "through the dust".  Can there be any true Christian ministry which is not diaconal, or through the dust?

## (3)    FRIEND

Really an extension of what I wrote about the priest as a human being.  Many of the Lancers are my friends, as well as people for whom I have been given some responsibility both by the Church and the Army.  The question is how far (whether in war or peace) the priest must be a professional person operating even-handedly in a spirit of clinical detachment;  and whether he can do so without anaesthetising a large part of his humanity to the point where it never wakes up.  The pitfalls are obvious.  Minefields abound – as if there aren't enough real ones already!  But I must try to see the creative factors, not just the dangers.

The Greeks had at least three words for love: *agape, philia, eros.*  In Christian usage these came to span far more meanings than the one word 'love' can really carry, ranging from the love of God himself, through various degrees of friendship, to erotic or sexual desire. I'm not sure we can keep them separate. I seem to find a bit of all of them in my relationships with the Lancers, and it is impossible to disentangle all the strands and motives. Anyway, are we really meant to do so?

The operative word from the gospels (though in a different context) is 'fear not'; at least, that is the word that comes to me. Don't be afraid of loving. The danger is not that your love will be too much – what a ridiculous thought – but that it will be too little and too selfish. Yet we all have to be ourselves, and if I am going to be me as I am, I will be drawn naturally to some more than to others. The real test is therefore over the others. *Agape* alone can help here, if we could only understand and enter into it. For there is nothing in that kind of love of self-gratification, getting something from others, even enjoying others; but working, living, if need be dying, for their well-being, simply because they too are human beings loved by God. And that in itself makes them friends, the friends for whom, St John says (15:13) that there can be no greater love than this, that you lay down your life for them. After all, I've seen it being done every day since D-Day, often by people who may never have heard of John 15:13.

If one can get that right, about the people to whom there is no strong natural attraction, all the rest is a bonus. Again, 'Fear not'. Why fear being attracted to the brave, the beautiful, the strong, the good? For the attraction is the sign of a spiritual connexion, a glimpse, tiny and fleeting it may be, of the goodness and beauty of God himself. Yet I am aware that that still leaves a number of questions unanswered. The trouble (joy?) is that there are no stock answers.

## (4)　　GO-BETWEEN

Much of my time is spent as a go-between: between the Regimental Aid Post in battle areas and medical stations further back; between commanded and commanders, with a ministry to both that makes the matter of rank irrelevant; between the Church at home and the Church here in the Army; between God and man, heaven and earth.

So one stands in between, in an uncomfortable ambiguity, but one full of creative possibilities. The difficulty is to stay in between, and not settle down into an identification with one element or another so complete as to wipe out the mediatorial, reconciling element. I must have heard lectures on the incarnation of Christ which might have helped me to sort this one out, but if I did I can't remember a word of them. In terms of prayer this mediatorial work is described as intercession. In theory, why should it need anyone to stand like Moses "in the gap" between God and the people? Can't he bestow his blessings without intermediaries? He can and he does; yet over and over again chooses rather to work through some human agency.

Those of us who are chaplains in battle have a tremendous opportunity of mediating Christ and his Church. So often the Church has a very inhuman, un-Christlike face. Pomp, power, privilege and possessions colour many people's perceptions, and not unfairly so. Out here, however, we are stripped of those things, and stripped also of most of the 'props' of Church life at home, so that we have nothing to do except what we were ordained to do, which is to represent Christ and his Church; to be with people in their pain as well as in their strength. (It is, incidentally, an extraordinary thing how happy and exhilarating life has been since D-Day despite the terrors and agonies.) Come to think of it, how are we chaplains going to accommodate ourselves to the unrealities of parish life after the war? Well, that's one thing I need not worry about at the moment.

## (5)    SACRIFICE

It sounds pompous, if not almost blasphemous, to say that all of us who are involved in these Normandy battles, British and Germans alike, are a sacrifice for sin. The phrase has strong theological overtones, but I use it unemotionally, factually, and for the moment non-religiously. For we, mostly young, have been thrown into war not because we chose it, but because of the mess that our nations, Great Britain and Germany, made of the twenty years that followed the ending of the 1914 war. We are therefore a sacrifice for sins in which we were too young to have much, if any, part: sins of compromise and cowardice on our side, and of militarism, racism and anti-semitism on Germany's part. This does not mean that we are morally as white as snow, simply that the sins of the fathers are, as ever, visited upon the children.

That is not, however, how most are looking upon it. Most people around me have a more prosaic philosophy of getting on with what has to be done. Yet for some, on both sides, there is something more positive than stoical endurance: in the opposing armies there are plenty of people who believe in the justice of their nation's cause strongly enough to embrace sacrifice, not just have it thrust upon them. This applies to many of the Lancers, even though they have been conscripted into the Forces, and it certainly applies to young Nazi teenage fanatics. Writing these things down thus baldly spells out the appalling tragedy and waste of war.

The Church is always having to operate in situations which are, to put it mildly, far from ideal. So it is now. One of the roles of the chaplain is therefore to be a participator in sacrifice, believing as I certainly do that there can be no peace with Nazi terror and tyranny. There is now no way on except by (literally) bloody sacrifice. For me, as I explained at the beginning of this diary, there is in this an element of expiation for my failure in walking out from Sandhurst in 1939, but I do not think of this aspect very much now. It is more a feeling that I must, and want to, identify myself with the offering that many are making, with no sheltering from danger behind non-combatant status. Then how does that square with driving around, as I sometimes do, with a red cross pennant flying from the wireless aerial of my vehicle? But if we take all these inconsistencies – hypocrisies some might call them – too seriously, we end up like paralysed rabbits, afraid to do anything.

Only in the context of Christian faith do these confusions and imperfections come together, never more so than in the Eucharist, where we plead the perfect sacrifice of Christ on the Cross, and put our imperfect offering alongside his, with acceptance sure, not because of our merits but through his advocacy.

## (6)   SIGN

The chaplain is, so I have found, a sign or symbol. A good regiment wants a chaplain, and commanding officers sometimes go to extreme, even unscrupulous, lengths to get a good one. If pressed for reasons, the answer would probably be to do with morale, a word greatly beloved by the Army.

It is easy to be cynical. Yes, they do want someone who will do welfare jobs, and do them well. Yes, they do want someone who will fit in, and relate easily to all ranks. Yes, they want someone who will take what they call a good service, and preach short sermons which are very much down to earth, yet steer clear of politics, or anything subversive. It is easy to say they want a kind of religious mascot, because in a way they do. But the English attitude to religion is always complex, and is rarely what it seems on the surface. At a deeper level there is often a yearning for something that won't go into words, and the chaplain, especially in war, is a sign or symbol of this hidden dimension. He is a sign or symbol of values that most hold dear, and which war cruelly contradicts, to do with home and love, with justice, peace, compassion, with beauty and creativity. The army padre does not need to keep speaking about these things. Just by being there he is a sign or reminder of them. He is not required to be a saint, in the non-biblical sense that that word has acquired, but it is vital that in him no coarseness, cruelty or contempt for others should set up a totally alien and unacceptable image. If anyone is in trouble, especially if it is of their own making, the chaplain must be the first to befriend them. This is expected by those in authority. Of course, he must do it in such a way as not to impair army discipline. That may be difficult, but it is part of the task for which the army has given him a recognised place in its complicated structure.

In all this he is a sign of a world beyond this one, and of the God whose ways are not our ways, and whose thoughts are not our thoughts. However far people have strayed from the faith in which they were brought up, I find that they welcome me as a sign of what they once cherished, and still, however vaguely, hope to attain. We despise and scorn these attitudes at enormous peril not only to the souls of those in our care, but our own souls also.

Re-reading these role reflections, I see that they are roles presented to me by circumstances, but my reflections on them are intermingled with ideals that I can only think are presented by God. Be that as it may, it has been important to try to set down what I have learnt about ordained ministry during the year I was with the Lancers in England, and even more in the weeks since D-Day. If I should ever be called on to train people for ministry after the war, I would want to go back to these headings – human being, servant, friend, go-between, sacrifice, sign – for I believe that even under quite different circumstances they could be equally relevant in peacetime.

I have been enjoying these few days at the Rest Camp, now coming to an end. I have even had a bath in Bayeux, an extraordinary open-air affair arranged by something I never knew existed, called an Army Bath Unit. Even more enjoyable were the vin blanc and calvados sampled with friends at the Lion D'Or and the Globe.

With HQ Officers of 4th/7th Royal Dragoon Guards. Somewhere between breaking out of Normandy and into Germany, 1944 - 45 *(Understandably tired!)*

## 18<sup>th</sup> July

In between bouts of deadly activity, war provides lulls which soon become boring. In some of these I am producing a news-sheet (in theory, weekly) called 'Lancer Life', with the aid of the orderly room staff in 'B' echelon. This has been a brilliant success, not because of the quality of the journalism but because it can't fail if it tells the members of a scattered regiment what is happening. As it often appears in battle that nobody from the top downwards has any idea what is happening, the editor is on to a winner, even if he doesn't know either.

The latest issue has an open letter of thanks from 45 Lancers to the Commandant of XXX Corps Rest Camp telling him of their tremendous appreciation of his efforts, memorial notes about people recently killed, and news of those recently wounded. This is probably the most important feature of all from a morale point of view. I have contributed an article entitled "R.I.P. at the R.A.P.", explaining the procedure for dealing with the wounded: "First a journey to the nearest Regimental Aid Post, where the M.O. will be tidying you up, but no big stuff, chopping off legs or anything like that; then by ambulance to the Casualty Clearing Point, perhaps a couple of miles back, where the very-nearly-dead are raised to almost certain new life by blood transfusions; eventually, via the Advanced Dressing Station, to a Casualty Clearing Station, which is complete with operating theatre, dental surgeon and real nurses. Here you might stay a couple of days before being shipped back to England." It all sounds a bit light-hearted in the article, but in fact what it describes does, miraculously, seem to happen. Not surprisingly, this issue has done a lot for the morale of Douglas

Aitken and his staff. Nobody knows better than me of their heroic, almost superhuman, labours since D-Day, and Douglas has at last been persuaded to go to the Corps Rest Camp himself – not before time.

## 19th July

All around us are extraordinary contrasts. There is the stunning beauty of the Normandy countryside in summer, with its lush green pastures, many orchards, woods, tall hedgerows: 'bocage' country in the French term - desperately unsuitable for tank warfare, which needs open country. By contrast with this idyllic scene are ruined houses and churches, the stench of dead cattle, cows lying dead with legs upstretched in *rigor mortis*; undiscovered corpses of English and German soldiers, eaten by maggots. Yet, strangely, the sense of beauty prevails, and we clutch at any sign of normality. For example, one of our chaps, a country boy, has been going twice a day to a nearby farm, evacuated but undamaged, tending the cattle, milking and watering them, shooting the wounded ones – and supplying the M.O. with milk and fresh eggs.

The British are much better at finding normality amid nightmare than at staging imaginative, daring, bloodthirsty battles. The hard slog and "if-you-know-of-a-better-'ole,-go-to-it" philosophy is much more our style – amazing that we ever win any wars. At the moment it doesn't much look as though we are going to win this one, though because nobody ever expresses that thought, we probably will.

I find to my shame that in my kit I have an embroidered altar cloth that I took some days ago from a bombed-out catholic church, meaning to return it after use.   Now I don't know that I will ever find the church, or even make the effort.   Better go easy on harsh sermons about the sins of looting!   Also, I exchanged the 2-stroke 'James' motor bike (quite useless in this countryside) for some butter from a French farmer, enough to butter much bread for many people.   Is this a sin?   Maybe not, but I've a nasty feeling that the War Office might take a different view.

### 23rd July

A bombshell:   news has come that the 24th Lancers are to be disbanded.   All of us will be scattered in the next week or two as reinforcements for other units, less than nine weeks after D-Day. This is certainly not because the regiment has failed, nor can it be because our casualties have been astronomical – about 50 killed and over 100 wounded;   bad enough, and God knows we have gone through enough pain in losing these friends, but it does not add up to a picture of utter decimation.   Cynically, we ask if the staff didn't jiggle units around like this, what would they do?

Poor 24th Lancers!   In a total of 150 years, from 1794 to 1944, they have had only twelve years of life:  first from 1794 to 1802, and then in 1940 resurrected through the parentage of the 9th Queen's Royal Lancers and the 17th/21st Lancers (the "Death or Glory Boys").   In the past four years the regiment has generated great *esprit de corps.* Its leaders have brilliantly combined tough discipline, professional efficiency of a high order, sensitivity to the needs of individuals, and a devil-may-care attitude that blasted its way in true cavalry style through pomposity and red tape, and made life enormous fun.   They made it seem like a family in which everyone counted, whatever their rank.   No wonder we are all shattered.

## 24th July

I tried to comfort the Colonel today, heartbroken as he is by the news. He is trying everything he knows to get the decision altered, but I think it is too late.

Lieutenant Colonel W.A.C. Anderson, universally known as WAC or more formally as Colonel WAC, is an outstanding leader. Aged 33, only six years older than me, he is, on the face of it, the typical hard-riding, hard-swearing cavalry officer full of aggressive energy and inexhaustible *élan*. His rebukes can be terrifying. He is capable of threatening drunken or ill-disciplined subalterns with being frog-marched in chains round the parade ground at dawn, with a bayonet up their behinds to speed progress – not that it ever happened, or not quite like that, and anyway WAC would have spoilt it all halfway through by inviting them to drinks and dinner that evening. Far from being a cavalry stereotype, he has eyes to weep and a heart that bleeds in the face of tragedy, and a poet's love of beauty. Back in England some months before the invasion, he gave me an 'Ode to a Country Boy' which he had cut out from the Sunday Times. The first verse went:

> How can it be in vain your morning sleeping,
> You who have died for all you love so much?
> Grassland and grain that ripened in your keeping
> Slow patient beasts that knew your gentle touch

It went on in that strain for four more verses. All this may make WAC sound like a sentimental and even dangerous idiot, but the fact is that he is loved throughout the Regiment for his utter professionalism and his colourful humanity.

A week or so after D-Day he was evacuated to England with severe injuries to his hand.    Having once got into the medical sausage machine he was swept inexorably across the Channel to a hospital in Southampton.   There it was found that he had broken several bones in his hand, but WAC soon escaped from hospital, and hitched a lift back to Normandy on a tank landing ship sailing from Portsmouth. Eventually, three days after leaving hospital, he found the Regiment and resumed command.   I was as glad as everyone else to see him back.   There can be few chaplains who have had greater support and understanding from their commanding officer.

I don't know how he would define his religious position.   I doubt if he would try to do so, but it must contain something of his native Scotland, though it is difficult to see what, because one's ideas of Scottish religion are pretty bleak -- probably a gross travesty.   But all the evidence is that the God WAC worships has creative energy and enormous love of life, knowing beauty, and enduring pain;   which is surely not a million miles away from orthodox faith in the God and Father of our Lord Jesus Christ.

### Sunday, 30th July

A large number came to this evening's farewell service:   all very simple, because it had to be in the open air.   I tried to inject a note of hope into what was inevitably a sad occasion, taking as a text, and out of context, Jesus' words at the end of the feeding of the five thousand as recorded by St John:   "Gather up the fragments that remain, that nothing be lost".   In the divine economy nothing is wasted.   The comradeship we have known in the Lancers, the experience gained, the fears overcome, the battles endured, the things we have done which we did not think we had it in us to do, none of this need be wasted.   There must be life beyond the 24th

Lancers! And I pointed out that our friends who have been killed in the last few weeks would urge us to go on and finish this war, and then, if spared, live to the full the life on earth denied to them; in a word, look back thankfully, and look forward hopefully. That was the sort of thing I said. It all looks pretty banal, set down like that, but (perhaps through tiredness) the uttering of these thoughts nearly reduced me to tears. Many people thanked me. On occasions like this there is a need for Wordsworth's 'thoughts that do lie too deep for tears' to be articulated by someone, however inadequately, in order that personal grief may be worked through.

Tonight there is a farewell party, and this week we shall all be scattered to different units. I was destined to join the 4th/7th Royal Dragoon Guards for the rest of the campaign.

Officers of the 4th/7th Royal Dragoon Guards being presented to Field-Marshal Sir Bernard Montgomery somewhere in northern Germany, June 1945, following V.E. day in May '45. *Mark Green is 2nd from right.*

# 31ˢᵗ July

This is certainly the end of a chapter, and I must apply my words of last night to myself. There are more lessons for the future than I can now recollect, but one line of thought especially strikes home.

Nobody would ever think of the Army, still less of war, as a school of spirituality. Yet so it has been for me, as I tried to spell out at the Rest Camp. This is all the more extraordinary because war is a cauldron seething with poisonous brews, which we all drink whether we want to or not. Their foulness dehumanises us; they destroy the beautiful; they twist truth by turning good into evil, and evil into good; they stir up blood lust, leaving a trail of broken minds and bodies; they bring death, pain and poverty to friend and foe alike. Non-combatant status does not make my hands clean. I have to face the fact that I support the killing, or I would not be here.

There is, however, another side to all this. For some people (and it is important not to exaggerate the number) war can have a refining effect, bringing forth an ascetic heroism which is one of the best fruits of all true religion.

I have seen it show itself so often in contempt for ease and safety, and in willingness to face suffering and death in devotion to a cause far beyond mere self-interest. The saving of others and concern for their wellbeing is quite commonplace in war, but is that not love at its highest, with no taint of possessiveness? In facing death, the soldier often sees what is most valuable in life. A letter from home, providing it does not contain bad news, is worth more than money. The loss of possessions counts for nothing compared with the gift of seeing the sun rise on a new day after a night of terror.

Thus there comes, at least to some, a conquest of self not utterly different from that depicted in the great classics of spirituality like Thomas à Kempis's *Imitation of Christ*. I happen to have been carrying a copy around with me in my kit, and reading bits of it at odd moments. Over and over again there are references to being 'set free from all attachment to earthly things', and on almost every page exhortations to endure sufferings and deprivation for the sake of what lies beyond. Of course, for Thomas à Kempis every self-denial is centred explicitly upon a desire to please God and draw near to heaven. Somewhere much lower down the holy mountain than Thomas, our heroic soldier is perhaps doing just that, though he would never express it like that. But is it not at least an antidote to the bitter brews we all drink from the cauldron of war?

These purgings of the soul can never be any kind of justification of war. It is tragic that it needs so much evil to bring out so much good. Like William James in his famous book *The Varieties of Religious Experience*, we need to ask whether there is not in the social realm what he calls the "moral equivalent of war" – something heroic that will speak to men as universally as war does, yet be as compatible with their spiritual selves as war, is incompatible, despite all that I have said ? How important it is for the human race to learn these lessons. We had better get on with it soon, for there is no ideal school of spirituality, whether in war or in peace, in the Church or outside it. The light of God is always filtered to our souls – if it is – through scenes of confusion and ambiguity. Here on earth we always, even at best, see through a glass darkly. The Christian hope is that in the end the true light will prevail. Meanwhile light has come in strange ways and through quite unexpected people during these weeks in Normandy.  Now at last, after all the hard slog since D-Day, there are signs of a breakthrough.

Mark Green,
*Chaplain with Far East Land Forces*
1953 - 1956

Mark Green with Archbishop Michael Ramsey,
outside Southwark Cathedral,
Ascension Day (Thursday 11th May) 1972,
after his consecration as Bishop of Aston.

This page represents
the passage of 59 years:
1944 - 2003

# WITHIN NO WALLS CONFINED

# 1. UNA KROLL

In February 2003 a lung scan showed the possibility of cancerous growth in one lung. Five months later (2 July 2003) another scan showed it had 'melted away' (consultant Dr James Wilkinson, Eastbourne District General Hospital, 9 July). No apparent reason, for no treatment had been applied.

Did I dance for joy?

No, my mind seemed blank. O God, can it be that in fact I wanted this cancer to have grown because really I wanted to die...? Wanted not to be alone much longer. My bags were packed and ready. Now I had to cope with life a bit longer.

Strange. Because if life is a gamble, death is even more so. Nothing is more final than a corpse. Deadness, corruption, decay; how can these be the doorways to life? Yet underneath death's door I see a chink of light. Gamble it may be but I'll go for it. Then a voice says, 'Don't talk about a gamble you've begun on the new life already.'

Certainly I have said this often enough to others, quoting John 5:24 for example: '... anyone who hears my word and believes him who sent me has eternal life, and does not come under judgement, but has passed from death to life'. Not only future but present. But at 86, with this physical life palpably receding, it is difficult not to focus on the future.

A letter in the *Times* today (14 July 2003) has helped me answer the question: reprieved (from cancer) *for what?* Una Kroll, now a priest in Monmouth was a militant campaigner for the ordination of women. Years ago she became notorious for chaining herself to the railings outside Church House, Westminster, probably during a meeting of the old Church Assembly. Some twenty years later I was surprised to find that I had been hearing her confessions at Christ Church, St. Leonards without knowing who she was; we used those old fashioned confessional boxes where the priest could see very little through the metal grille (he wasn't meant to) and I only heard a little, because I had to sit with a slightly deaf ear towards the grille. So it was sometimes a matter of making up the sins for which one then declared God's forgiveness to the penitent.

Gradually I got to know Una outside the 'box'. Her wisdom, gentleness and kindness made a great impression on me. Not once did she challenge my views (then) against the ordination of women or seek to convert me. When the General Synod voted in favour (November 1992) I said to Una that I assumed she would be one of the first. No, she replied, she would only be ordained if her bishop asked her. He did (Rowan Williams). She was. In her letter today she affirms her respect for his integrity and decisions, even when she did not agree with them. But she deplored the decision recently made not to proceed with the appointment of the gay priest Jeffrey John to the bishopric of Reading: 'Thus honesty is punished and secrecy supported. Who would want to join a church that has become obsessed with what should be a completely marginal matter compared with the big issues of poverty, cruelty and injustice? The answer is that many decent people don't want to join the church; and I, who already belong, do not want to stay. But I am not going to leave. I am going to do what I can to encourage Christians to look at the issues of integrity which result in economic and social injustice in our world. I hope that many other quite ordinary, economically weak and apparently powerless Christians will do the same.' I agree totally with what Una has written.

*\*\**

So what can I do about it Lord? Not a lot at 86 perhaps. But whether I have a year or two more, or perhaps only a few months, please show me your way before I go. One thing I can do is to write as honestly as possible about the tasks facing Christians in England - and in Europe generally - and I have to begin by expressing dismay. Maybe I have thought overmuch about our failure. Yes, it is my failure, too, because I have been in positions of leadership these last decades. Now there is an emptiness and dullness about many Christian gatherings. There is alienation from the people and estrangement from your gospel of love and service to the poor. And where, Lord, are your prophets? Our bishops are often reduced to being managers of an increasingly bureaucratic institution, with so many committees that prophecy is smothered. All that, and more about your Church, which I hate and yet love so much. I cannot die without it.

Let me help others to see further: that we are not confined to an increasingly irrelevant structure in a dying institution. Your Spirit fills the world. Where can we flee from your presence even if we want to? *'For thou, within no walls confined inhabitest the humble mind'* (NEH 390, William Cowper 1731-1800)

So you give healing to the sick, release to the prisoners, you speak peace to the nations and give courage and hope to the young.

All this spills over from our 'walls confined' into the world where your Spirit knows no boundaries of race or religion. *There* are your people, your instruments of love and peace, following your servants Francis and the Teresas and so many others - servants of your kingdom, whether they know it or not.

*Praise to you dear God. You are always doing a new thing. Help us to do it with you and use even me before I go, to write words that might start somebody on your new path, making a way in the wilderness and rivers in the desert.*

*Amen.*

## 2. NORMANDY CADET PILGRIMAGE

God began almost immediately to unfold the prayer that ended the last section, and spelt out some of its implications for me, and indeed for the whole Church. This was through a cadet pilgrimage to the Normandy invasion areas, 25-28 July, 2003.

As Chaplain to the Royal British Legion in Eastbourne, I initiated two years ago a series of cadet unit pilgrimages to the world war battlefields. We thought of it as a gesture of friendship from ageing war veterans to the young of today, and raised the necessary funds.

Exactly how I would explain my involvement at any deeper level, I'm not sure. It was not a conscious effort to turn these boys and girls into Christians, which some of them (by no means all) are already. It was, and is, more a case of helping them to be fulfilled as human beings - perceiving dragons needing to be slain if our world is to survive.

In Caen there is a huge Museum of Peace, visited as part of our pilgrimage. All round the city are signs pointing the way to 'Le Memorial de Caen.' On many of them are the words: *HISTOIRE POUR COMPRENDRE LE MONDE.* That's it exactly: to help the young understand the world they've inherited.

These pilgrimages make a big impression, bringing home, more than any history lesson can do, the horror and waste of war. The word or idea that jumps out and hits them is SACRIFICE: the sacrifice of millions of (mainly young) people of all nations in the slaughter of war. To what purpose? They will have to spend the rest of their lives working out the answer if they can; and if they can't there may not be a world as we know it to understand. But meanwhile - blessed word, because there is still a meanwhile for most of us whatever our circumstances - meanwhile they made a positive act of remembrance and dedication in the Bayeux British and Commonwealth War Cemetery with its 4,500 graves. This was not something I imposed on the programme. It got itself there by the mutual unspoken understanding of all involved that this would be the central point of the four day pilgrimage.

I noted with interest how they played it. Everybody travelled in ordinary clothes for the whole tour except for this one short ceremony. For this they changed into uniform on the coach, which was parked on the main road outside the cemetery. (Curtains discreetly drawn, girls first, then boys). I also put on uniform: robes liturgically incorrect but visually communicative, an alb, multicoloured stole, purple skull cap. pectoral cross.

The cadets marched with perfect drill and discipline from the road to the large white cross at the far end of the cemetery. At 10.a.m on a Sunday morning there were only three visitors there. No question, then, of doing this march in front of an admiring crowd, but they could just as well have done it in front of the Queen on Horse Guards Parade. One of the girls read beautifully from the last chapter of Paul's letter to the Church in Ephesus: *'Put on the whole armour of God....for our struggle is against the spiritual forces of evil....Take the shield of faith and the sword of the Spirit which is the word of God.'* I followed this with a brief recollection of the first days of the 1944 Normandy invasion: the extraordinary contrast between the stench of death (men and cattle) and the stunning beauty of the Normandy countryside in early summer: death and destruction versus beauty, courage, and self-sacrifice. And the world is still the same, for we have the same contrasts and conflicts even if they are covered much of the time with a smattering of civilization. The point of these pilgrimages is not to dwell on the past, but to reflect on what the past is telling us about our lives and the future. It was important for each one there that morning to face that question. That was all, and our ceremony closed with the laying of a poppy wreath, silence, a prayer and finally handing over the Royal British Legion's Torch of Remembrance to representative cadets, with a blessing.

This weekend I have broken away from the established routine of the Church, for our pilgrimage had nothing officially to do with the Church. It has opened my mind again to the question: where are Christians, ordained and lay, meant to be operating? The answer must be in many places and situations other than, and in addition to, parish churches.

In our own church, for example, we have four Readers and several retired clergy. There is no real ministry for most of them within the walls of the church, but enormous need and scope outside. Some are certainly developing these possibilities.

For myself, I'm lucky. In the coach on the way back to Eastbourne I told the cadets and their leaders that not many people of 86 have the opportunity of doing a tour like the one we'd just done, and doing it with such wonderful people. Some unkind person might have added that not many at that age would be mad enough to want to. In which case my answer could only be that I'm glad to be mad.

* * *

Thank you, Lord, for a glimpse of the goodness of the young given to me in those Normandy days. As 60 years ago, when evil and beauty fought for life, so now these children of a sated, overfed part of the world, learn that there can be no victory of your Spirit without conflict and sacrifice. But thank you, Lord, for their beauty, bravery, and love. May each take from Bayeux Cemetery the words given them there: -

**I WILL BE BRAVE**

TO
$$\left. \begin{array}{l} \textbf{FIGHT} \\ \textbf{LIVE} \\ \textbf{LOVE} \end{array} \right\}$$
FOR OTHERS

## 3. WHY I CANNOT LEAVE THE CHURCH

Many have done so for a variety of reasons. The ordination of women, and now the same question about gay people. Many have left because they feel the institutional church is out of touch with the real world. But most because it is just plain boring. I wouldn't be able to leave because I would know that I was flinging back in God's face a great gift. His Church has come to me not as a demand, requiring mental contortions to believe the gospel; nor to take on a regime requiring seven impossible things to be done every day, but as a *gift*, with unconditional love.

Oscar Wilde said: ' Education is an admirable thing. But it is well to remember from time to time that nothing worth knowing can be taught'. Certainly my faith was caught rather than taught. I caught it initially from my parents: Ernest (by the time I was born he was ordained and a regular Army Chaplain) from a Victorian evangelical background where novel reading was banned on Sundays, and theatre-going always, and alcohol simply meant supping with the Devil; Miranda from an Anglo-Catholic family, familiar with 'bells and smells' on good terms with God through regular confession and communion. Neither of them gave me any explicit religious teaching that I can remember, though I do remember family prayers before breakfast, probably with a bible-reading - the whole thing short and interesting. Both parents had come from their strong religious backgrounds to a marriage that often tottered on the brink, but was held up by a faith that was not only firm, but fun.

As to formal religious education, either I had none, no Sunday school for example, or it washed over me harmlessly in what were then called 'divinity lessons ' at school. Even the confirmation classes that my sister and I received from a neighbouring vicar were quite meaningless, and only came to life at the end of the lesson when he gave us a boiled sweet known as a bulls-eye. He then got us to our knees for prayer, when I disgraced myself by getting the giggles and nearly choking to death on the bulls-eye. The confirmation itself, of the two of us and two others on a weekday morning in his cathedral (by the Bishop of Lichfield), was a different matter. That came as a gift that was, and is, miraculously renewable.

Sooner or later the faith that is somehow breathed into a child has to be owned and exercised. My father's last gift to me came, in a strange way, after his death in 1936 from pneumonia aged 55. Not knowing what else to do when I left school, I accepted the help of a young barrister friend of the family, Peter Thorneycroft (later to become Harold Macmillan's Chancellor of the Exchequer), in becoming articled to a firm of Birmingham solicitors. But after Ernest's death, as I read his diaries and reflected on his ministry, I saw how beautiful it was compared with what I was doing. One day, as I cycled home from Chipping Campden station after a day in Birmingham, on a sudden impulse I stopped at the Vicarage, our former home, and asked the new Vicar how one set about being ordained. My father had never even suggested this, far less put any pressure on me to follow in his footsteps, but I reckon that the ministry on which I eventually entered was not only God's gift, but his.

Has it been a handicap to my ministry that I have not had to struggle, as many do, with obstacles to belief in a loving God? The answer must be that, as for some of them, my faith has been tested in the horror of battle, and the squalor and indignity of death, especially of beautiful people, and young people.

But whereas my spiritual journey has been from the Church into the world, many today start from the world into.......well, into what? So much both in the world and in the Church contradicts the God of love. Thus people make up a religion of their own, often bearing some resemblance to the one embodied by Jesus of Nazareth, which they hope immunises them against so-called religious people, and the worst practices of the Church.

Thus it may be that the most vital kind of ministry today is in the secular world, helping the many who search for ultimate meaning in life and death. The help they most need is to find a way of belonging to Christ's body, for without that union we become like dried up branches cut off from the tree

Lord, thank you for your Church.

Thanks that it was not formed by a committee,
recruiting like-minded people to continue your work.
Thanks indeed that it wasn't really an organisation,
more an explosion, life bursting out of the tomb,
convincing the apostles that you were not death's prisoner,
but really alive after they knew you were really dead and buried.
They carried that message from Jerusalem.
It spread like fire fanned by your Spirit,
till it reached the ends of the earth.
Thanks that through the centuries the fire has never quite gone out,
in spite of corruption, betrayal, conflict and persecution.
It is still your Body, divine as well as human.
Like any body, it must grow and change,[1]
so must we,
'always carrying in the body the death of Jesus,
so that the life of Jesus may also be made visible in our bodies'[2]
*'As dying, and behold we live!'*[3]

[1] *Here below is to change and to be perfect is to have changed often*
John Henry Newman

[2] 2 Corinthians 4:9          [3] 2 Corinthians 6:9

## 4. MINISTRY BEYOND THE WALLS

### A Christmas Letter 2003

(For the last 15 years I have sent a Christmas letter to some 150-200 friends, mostly living away from Eastbourne)

Each Christmas as I do these letters I wonder if this one will be the last. Meanwhile, I survive, despite (or perhaps because of) having given up the car after Easter. I felt I was really an accident waiting to happen; so, prompted by a nice little accident with charming people a year ago (on the way back from the Crematorium so no question of drink!), I realised the next one would probably not be so charming. Thanks to friends it has been easier than I thought, and I still have been able to travel a bit: Cyprus (wonderful), Majorca (never again), and Normandy (deeply moving).

Stupidly, I had thought that in my 21$^{st}$ year of retirement I had nothing more to prove. I think God probably enjoys having this sort of laugh and he had this one on me. He must have prompted Kevin Bell, a friend from my Birmingham days, to phone me with a difficult request. He is now a Chaplain in the Army: 'Senior Chaplain Soldier Training' is his title. He explained that he was organising a conference for chaplains from all over the UK on the 'Chaplain in Battle' and he invited me to give two lectures on the last day of this three-day conference, one of them on the 'Moral Components of Fighting Power'. He gave me a specimen list of six such components: loyalty, courage, integrity, discipline, respect for others, selfless commitment. All this was to be at the Armed Forces' Chaplaincy Centre, Amport House near Andover.

Naturally I fell for it, though it was at once obvious that these moral components conflict sharply with the sort of culture in which most

57

of the young grow up today. But it is a most important issue, not only for service chaplains, but for the whole Church, and indeed the nation. Came the day when, last May, I arrived at Amport House, understandably nervous. Kevin in the course of introducing me said 'Bishop Mark is 87, but......' Probably he was about to add 'not yet totally ga-ga', but I chimed in: 'Hi, Kevin, don't pile it on, I'm only 86'. This got us off to a good start, and I was encouraged by the summary he sent me some weeks later of the evaluation sheets the participants had filled in after the speakers had gone.

\* \* \*

A spin-off from that conference was an invitation to repeat one of my talks to young Royal Engineering Officers at the Royal School of Military Engineering in Chatham. So a month later I did. Well, not quite, because the Amport House audience was entirely composed of clergy, and the Royal Engineers were entirely lay people. This group of about 25 were all recently commissioned from Sandhurst, all in their early twenties. Their specialist training at Chatham avowedly includes moral development 'with the aim of exposing them to some of the moral dilemmas and issues they might expect to face in war' - I quote from their Commanding Officer's letter of invitation.

What an impressive group it was that I addressed on that June afternoon. Any profession that can attract recruits of the calibre of those young men has nothing to fear. I shared with them some of the moral dilemmas they will undoubtedly face, not only in scenes of war and violence. Their response showed that the Army today does not want brainless, heartless fighting machines, but warm, intelligent human beings like this lot.

Behind all this is the work of their chaplain, Bob Green. Through him and through the chaplains I met at Amport House I got a glimpse of the Church working on the frontiers of the secular world. They are ministering to huge numbers of younger people who are missing from most churches. The interface between secular culture and spiritual commitment is a dangerous no-man's land. It is all too easy for the authorities to see religion as a useful tool, rather than the mystery it is, calling us in to realms unknown. But it is in that dangerous sphere that Christian mission will have its cutting edge, more than in parish churches often deserted except for a handful of the faithful retired.

The truth may be that the parochial structure is finished in its present form, without changes that at present those in charge dare not make and those in the pews would not accept. Who said 'God buries his workmen and carries on his work'? I don't know. But it is of course the story of Christmas: the old Israel gives way to the new: a new covenant, a new law, a new start. 'Behold I am doing a new thing' (Isaiah 43:19) is God's perpetual theme. May you share my recent experience of seeing what that might mean.

# 5A. LAST CONFIRMATIONS ?

May, 2004

The last ones?   Yes, I know, never say never, it's usually wrong. But within sight of being ninety I can't see myself doing another confirmation like the one I did at Worth Abbey, near Crawley, last month: 50 to confirm, with a congregation of 600, in that huge modern (1960's) circular building. I got through, in more senses than one, but it tested me to the limits of physical stamina, and I had to call in aid every bit of spiritual capital I possess, in the sort of way described in the sermon that follows.

Most of all it was a test of communication. As it happened, the Sunday before, I had been called to do a confirmation at Mayfield, near Tunbridge Wells, mainly for the convent (girls) school there, St. Leonard's Mayfield. Worth also has a much respected convent (boys) school. Two convent schools in a week! Money for old rope, you might think. Just dish out a few religious platitudes souped up a bit for monks and nuns, and what are you worrying about? Well I'm not quite as stupid as that. Call them what you will - religious communities, parishioners, teenage pupils, parents, teachers - they are as sophisticated as they come, yet, strangely by today's worldly standards, humble and hungry for the truth. Communicating with such people is not the Church of England's strongest point.

St. Dunstan's, Mayfield is a typical wealthy Sussex parish, the sort of place where it takes a real saint of a vicar to <u>stop</u> people going to Church! I have preached and done confirmations there several times over the past ten years, and was never very happy with it. Preaching there was like punching a bag full of stones or bottles. Many had made a definite mark in life, in education, the law, the armed forces, politics, and so on. Long-Service-and-Good-Conduct medals (OBE's etc..) dangled metaphorically on their chests. Previous visits had left me with a sense of failure, of not connecting.

But last month it was different. They sparked up, laughed, listened. I think the truth was not that they had changed, but that I had. On earlier visits I had dressed them in garments of honour, and forgotten the inner humanity and longing, the sorrows, sinfulness and loneliness which bind me with them. I see it all now. Why not before? (More worryingly, what am I still not seeing?)

There was a week between Mayfield and Worth. Although it had gone well, I decided not to repeat the Mayfield sermon at Worth. Sometimes circumstances compel repetition, but each occasion calls for a fresh brew, not a heated up repetition. More about Worth later, but now I want to focus on **COMMUNICATION.**

Preaching is always costly and draining, and if it isn't, it isn't worth doing. To think your message into a communication that will actually reach anyone means excluding many of the ideas that pour into your mind as you consider your theme.

Long ago, on joining the Royal Army Chaplains Department in World War 2 as a young newly-ordained priest, I was sent on a three-week school for Chaplains at Tidworth. Frank Woods, the Commandant (later Bishop of Middleton), gave us a lecture on preaching; I didn't know that I was about to be pitchforked into Colchester Garrison for three months of basic training under a senior chaplain. The most memorable part of this was having to preach on many Sunday mornings at Parade Service in Colchester Garrison Church. Some 500 young soldiers would have been marched there whether they wanted to worship or not. If they got bored with the sermon, which with me was very quickly, they had a way of bringing it to an end by all developing a hacking cough, not implausible in the month of February!

But back to Tidworth: Frank Woods's lecture on preaching gave us some tests to apply to our sermons. The only one I remember, maybe the most important one, was *Was its main point memorable?* Many sermons today would fail this test because they don't have a main point, or indeed any point at all, for they are just poorish essays read out to bored congregations.

For there to be real communication it is not the words written on paper as you prepare that matter; they matter only in so far as the process of writing helps to clarify your thoughts. It's the Word with a capital W written on your heart by God for *these* people on *this* occasion which will transfer itself from you to them; more accurately from God to them. To be a servant of the Word is a costly ministry.

*  *  *

If these are to be two of the last confirmations I do, I must be happy that both of them made some impact.

Father David Jarmy (chaplain) wrote after the one at Worth saying: 'One of the boys, who had decided *not* to be confirmed, came along to support his friends. His parents told me how moved and inspired he was - the most "moving experience he had ever had" - and how he wished he could have 'come up', and said he had changed his mind!' David said he should have done so, and that neither he nor I would have been too fazed by it. No, indeed.

This raises an important question about the age for confirmation. Father David, (who is half-time Vicar of Turners Hill, Crawley, and half-time Anglican Chaplain at Worth) had invited me to visit the group of boys during the week before the Confirmation Sunday.

All of them were in Year 10 (15 years old), and he told me he does not prepare or present candidates younger than this. These mid-teenage boys were relaxed with him; and at their ease with me, despite an age gap of approximately 72 years! (87-15) There was no fixed programme, but they kept me for an hour. We just chatted. They probed a bit to see where I was, and had the knack of making me respond, even if only to admit uncertainty; in fact they treated me as a human being, sometimes needing help just like them. Naturally I warmed to them. Who wouldn't? If only relationships were more like this in the church at large! And how much it says for the Church at Worth Abbey that the Anglican minority can be entirely at ease in a Roman Catholic establishment. Please God, a sign of things to come! My encounter with this group reinforced my belief that we have got into a considerable muddle over confirmation. Thirty and more years as a bishop have taught me that there is no right age to be confirmed, but that there is a wrong age. If confirmation has been truly described (as I think it has) as the 'ordination of the laity,' then it is ridiculous to confirm children below teenage. Admit them to communion-yes, of course, after due preparation and hopefully with family backing. But if confirmation is not so much a completion of baptism as a fulfilling of it, and a sending out with the gifts of the Spirit to fight Christ's battles in the world, then the Worth School practice of not confirming below the age of 15 is absolutely right.

I hope the sermon I preached that Sunday afternoon at Worth Abbey, printed below, puts flesh and blood onto what I have just written. So much depends for the vigour and effectiveness of the Christian mission in this country on inspiring, empowering, and firing the young with passion for Christ and his gospel.

## 5B. YOU, TOO, CAN BE VERY RICH
### The sermon at the Confirmation in Worth Abbey, Sunday May 9, 2004

*Those who wait for the Lord shall renew their strength,*
*They shall mount up with wings as eagles,*
*They shall run and not be weary,*
*They shall walk and not faint (Isaiah 40: 31)*

Isn't that the wrong order? No. The natural order is walk/run/mount up - if you do. But God's order, the spiritual order is the other way round:

*They shall mount up with wings as eagles*

First, some vision,

When you're young, if you don't have a gleam in your eye, if you don't have someone or something you would die for - even if it's only Arsenal or Chelsea or Aston Villa - there is something wrong. If there's no passion, no vision of the nations living at peace in a world of justice, no fire in your belly, then you're half dead already, just an expensive eating machine. As the Lord renews your strength today you will 'mount up with wings as eagles'. But then comes the testing middle part of life, and the second promise: *They shall run and not be weary.* That middle part really goes from the early twenties until you are about 60, and it is over those years that you are stretched to the utmost limit, not only stretched but stressed; working long hours, up at 6.30, away by 7.15, back exhausted in the evening... where's that soaring vision to help you run in the heat of the day and endure the conflicts, see what matters and what doesn't, be true to those who love you and need you?

* * *

And then...*They shall not walk and not faint* - in the desert of old age, 'the loneliness of the long distance runner', with failing health, and loved ones gone but keeping right on to the end of the road.

These are God's promises for every stage of our journey. I may have made it sound rather bleak, but it does require strength and courage. And it is God's gifts, God's promises, that we celebrate at this Eucharist, and every Eucharist and confirmation. You are going to affirm for yourself the promises made at your baptism. But God's promises and gifts to us are greater than ours to him. One of the most beautiful prayers I ever say privately or publicly is the one for the gifts of the Spirit for those about to be confirmed:

'Let your Holy Spirit rest upon them.
The Spirit of **wisdom and understanding, right judgement and courage,**
**knowledge and reverence,** the Spirit of **wonder and awe**'
seven wonderful gifts!

It is like being given a cheque for a huge sum. But the cheque won't be any use unless you do something about it. I mean, it's no use being given the Spirit of courage unless you are going to be given situations where courage is needed. Are you ready for that? And the more you spend, the more will be in your bank account. Did you ever hear of a bank where your balance increases the more you spend, and conversely, decreases and vanishes if you don't use it? You 've got to cash the money in. You've got to *use* those gifts. Like many,  I had to learn the hard way.

Sixty years ago Europe was in the grip of a cruel, evil regime. In 1944 there took place what has been described as the 'most stupendous enterprise in the history of warfare, and the most successful military deception since the Trojan Horse'. I was chaplain to an armoured brigade and attached to the 24th Lancers. I often wondered how I would cope, having had a rather sheltered existence. I could hardly summon up the courage to take a dead mouse out of a mousetrap, so how would I cope with dead bodies, especially (though I hadn't foreseen this) having to scrape them off the floor of a Sherman tank? But 'great your strength if great your need', and one surprising thing about those first days in Normandy was an extraordinary sense of exhilaration. I've never felt so alive before or since, and that was true for many in my unit. It wasn't bloodthirstiness or anything like it. It wasn't just animal energy or high spirits; it was God. It was a Presence, a power beyond our own. Perhaps not so surprising . After all, the lives of so many innocent people were at stake. Many of us felt closer to God in Normandy perhaps than we had felt in churches at home. No communion services have ever been so meaningful to me as those we held in strange circumstances.

I wasn't the only one who was cashing in every bit of spiritual capital I had.

So it must be - not, please God, in another world war - but we do face a world torn apart by hatred and greed, and ruled by fear; and one in which so many are in great need of food and medicine, of shelter and the ability to live their lives with dignity in freedom.

I started with Isaiah, and I'll finish with other words from his book, (Chapter 6) when he had a vision of God, high and lifted up in the Temple

> *Then I heard the voice of the Lord saying*
> *'Whom shall I send, and who will go for us?'*
> *And I said 'Here am I-send me'*

Please, God, someone here today might answer in the same way:

*Here I am, Lord. Is it I Lord?*
*I have heard you calling in the night*
*I will go, Lord if you lead me.*
*I will hold your people in my heart.*

As you go, God bless you and give you his strength.

## 6. FROM THE HOUSE OF KINGS TO THE COURTS OF HEAVEN
### A Christmas letter, 2004


Well, I'm still here, just about. Still living a reasonably normal life, though emphysema takes its toll with breathlessness and exhaustion. But I still know my own name and am still privileged to preach in Eastbourne's ancient parish church, where people have an astonishing tendency to listen to sermons as if they were actually going to receive something valuable! And of course they do. The pangs of old age are one thing, when you have to be ready to go and then are told to wait. The birth pangs of a new age are another. The world groans with pain as we try to cope with fear, need and greed. The Church, too, has to cope with a kind of death, our credibility running out daily. Often this dying has been a prelude to resurrection, and I believe it will be so again, so don't let them hammer our coffin lid down too soon. The corpse has a way of sitting up and jumping out! 'Behold, I am doing a new thing' is God's eternal watchword as we wait for a new birth, a new creation (*Isaiah* 43:19).

I ask myself, as no doubt you do, what and where are the signs of this new age? The answer came to me in London yesterday, in a strange way.

* * *

Having time to fill in I went to Westminster Abbey, intending to sit down in the nave and think a bit. ' Sorry, Sir, (Sir!) no entrance this way' said a red-gowned man at the west door, 'go round that corner and along the path to the tourist entrance'. A narrow entrance indeed, with a notice over a cash desk, £7 for entrance, £5 for pensioners etc. I was about to say to the girl cashier ' I'm a bishop and all I wanted to do was to pray'...Ouch! Fortunately I didn't and said 'What I really want to do is to sit down'. As her hand went to the ticket machine I turned away, but she called me back and gave me a ticket which said:

Price: £0.00     Visitor Type: Guest

Much ashamed of myself, I went in, and (not intending to break any rules) found myself within a cordoned-off area in the choir (not a tourist in sight!). I turned westwards towards the nave, out of the choir, and came to a stop behind the nave altar, still cordoned off. Wondering how to escape with dignity I looked down and saw that I was standing on a memorial stone. Reading the inscription, I was amazed to see that I was standing on the memorial to a dear friend. Here is its wording:

### ERIC SYMES ABBOTT, KCVO
### 1906 - 1983
### DEAN OF WESTMINSTER, 1959-1974
### FRIEND AND COUNSELLOR OF MANY.
### HE LOVED THE CHURCH OF ENGLAND
### STRIVING TO MAKE THIS HOUSE OF KINGS
### A PLACE OF PILGRIMAGE AND PRAYER FOR ALL
### PEOPLES

### PASTOR PASTORUM

I was one of the many to whom Eric Abbott was a friend and counsellor. He was one of the most formative influences on my life and ministry for about 25 years. And now I was standing on his memorial, perhaps over his ashes.

More than that, I suddenly saw in the simple yet sublime words of the Inscription the hallmarks of the new age to which God is leading his Church, with all the pain that belongs to new birth.

The first of these hallmarks must be INCLUSION. Just as Eric Abbott strove to make the Abbey a place of pilgrimage and prayer *for all peoples*, so it must be for the whole Church today. Yet the Anglican Communion is beginning to break up as strong, strident elements call for homosexuals to be excluded from ordination and women from becoming bishops.

If God really condemns gays - who didn't, after all, choose their nature - simply because they express their love, I wouldn't want to worship him. The test Jesus would surely apply to us, as to all, is not 'how much do you conform to the Mosaic Law?' but 'how much does your love cost in fidelity and self-giving?'

The other issue, the ordination of women as bishops, presents enormous difficulties. Our Church decided twelve years ago to ordain women as priests and there are now large numbers of them. There can be no going back. Logically some must in due course become bishops. The solution is not to find or found an alternative church. Somehow we must learn to live together in the one we've got. But inclusion, or communion (a better word), will not be without pain. Has it ever been so.

*  *  *

The other hallmark is TRANSCENDENCE. Eric Abbott wanted people of all kinds to find the Abbey " a place of pilgrimage and prayer". Much in our daily life drags us down, and many who are outside the church or on its edges look for that which transcends the violence of the battle-field, the squalor of the gutter, and the greed of the market-place. The word 'pilgrimage ' on Eric's memorial stone reminds us all that we can't stay in that 'House of Kings' but must move out and move on to find 'transcendence' in some unlikely spheres: I'm thinking of such places as a hospice for dying children where there is Life in the midst of death; a Church Secondary School I know where a lot of pupils receive communion who hardly ever enter a church; a theatre or concert hall where drama, music or ballet lift people into realms unknown, unvisited before; a prison where God's ministers proclaim liberty to the captives; and, not least, cathedrals which, like Westminster Abbey are often the most powerful mission centres in England

\* \* \*

In some ways old age is rather like being in the departure lounge of an airport, waiting around - hard to settle down to anything. For the umpteenth time you scan the departures on the screen above to see what's happening to your flight. The answer is nothing. So another cup of coffee, or another attempt to settle down to reading that Dickens novel you keep putting down at home because there's no time. Or even think about a sermon you have to preach on the Sunday after you get back...Something's coming up on the board about my flight so I must go... No, it's delayed again. More waiting... Might even start on that Christmas letter. Take care. Don't lose heart. Don't miss *your* flight! Meanwhile really enjoy Christmas.